SEEKING REFUGE

AN UNSUNG STORY OF KASHMIRI PANDITS

YUTIKA RAJANAK

Made with ♥ on the Notion Press Platform
www.notionpress.com

Contents

Contents

Author's Address

Through this book, I want to describe the story of the valley of Kashmir taking you back into the year 1990 after which things were never the same again for the people of the Kashmiri Pandit community who peacefully lived in the valley once. What draws my deepest interest in writing about this topic is the fact that I myself am a Kashmiri Pandit. I was born more than a decade after the unfortunate exodus of Kashmiri Pandits from their homeland to scatter themselves in not only different parts of the country but, all across the globe making them refugees in their own country. With this book, I would like to express and put in front of the readers the story of what such happened back in the year 1990 because of which the heart of every Kashmiri Pandit aches till date. I have grown up to listen to the stories told by my parents and grandparents about how the migration took place and how did terror take over the mind and heart of every Kashmiri Pandit at that time and still continues to. Hence, I make an attempt to describe this story to all my readers to the fullest of my potential as it is a story that is really close to my heart. Presenting to you a story of irrevocable sacrifice, terror, bloodshed and loss, a story of courage and strength, presenting to you a story of KASHMIR and the KASHMIRI PANDITS.

Preface

SEEKING REFUGE is a story that revolves around the year 1990. It talks about how the clouds of terrorism started surrounding the valley of Kashmir and brought about a change in the lives of the people of the Kashmiri Pandit community who lived there. Right from its appearance on the mighty land of ' India', Kashmir has nurtured people of all faiths with no malice for any culture or community. This serenity of Kashmir was the inspiration behind emperor Shah Jahan quoting it as " Heaven on Earth". Since centuries, the inhabitants of Kashmir lived in immense harmony and brotherhood irrespective of cultural and religious interests. But alas, what happened in this sacred and humanitarian valley of Kashmir is still hard to believe. It became a nightmare for the ancient and peaceful community of 'Kashmiri Pandits' who became scapegoats. The book describes the misery of the Kashmiri Pandits and how the horrific incidents that took place over there back in the year 1990 made them leave their homeland after which their life took a drastic turn and they still continue to struggle to face the situations that they find themselves in today.

CHAPTER ONE

THE DREARY NIGHT

Amidst the foggy woods on a late winter night, they could be seen loading items of necessity and some furniture in a huge truck. The trunks, the bags, all of them filled with things that they needed to live in a different place and yet leaving behind their soul and life in that house of the valley of Kashmir. To them, it was not merely a night, not merely a house, not merely a place, it was their soul that ached seeing themselves leave the valley which to them was their whole life in the lap of which they wished to spend their last breath. Among all the other things that bothered them, the very question that whether they would ever be able to return or not, pricked them but they had to keep going because if the sun shone and they were seen by the militants, they would be killed in fraction of a minute. Yes, the night was dark, not because it was the night time, but because they were leaving behind all they had always wished for, MEMORIES OF KASHMIR. The place they had wanted to take their last breath in, had to be left now and it was finally time as they could have risked their lives and become a prey to gun shots even if they stood there for a day more. They were a family of nine with grandparents, their two sons, Anand and Ambar married to Megha and Naina respectively who were equally aching because their parents had already left the last night. Anand and Megha had two sons named Rohan who was 15 years old and Varun who was 8 years old whereas Ambar and Naina had a daughter who was a four year old little girl named Neha. With immense terror in their heart, Anand and Ambar were loading a few clothes in the truck when all of them heard a loud noise. A yet another Kashmiri pandit's house in the next street had been burnt by the militants and all the family members were killed ruthlessly. They now knew that they had to leave as soon as possible so they left all the other belongings and all sat in the truck and left as staying even for a few more minutes would mean death. All their family photos and memories, they left in their house but carried them along in their hearts forever. They left. Yes, they did. Leaving that huge house, big gardens and lawns, the fruits that grew in them and all that essence of belongingness that they had for the land they were born in, they left to seek refuge somewhere in their own country and to become a refugee in their own country. It was not just them but the lakhs of Kashmiri Pandits who left the valley and migrated to different places in the country to seek refuge because they were brutally killed in their own land by the militants who entered their house and killed them and hence, capturing their houses. Not just did this family feel the pain of separation from their land, but there were lakhs of other Kashmiri pandits who suffered from this pain of separation. The night was dark and cold, and these families had no clue as to what hardship awaited them. The children slept, but the elders were awake. How could they sleep? The grandmother cried, and she kept on weeping. Nobody stopped her. How could they. She had spent her whole life in the valley. She was a daughter of the valley. While going, all she had in her mind were the memories of Kashmir, all the days she had spent there and all the fun she had had there ever since her childhood.

CHAPTER TWO

THE FLASHBACK!!

All of them were awake with their heads leaned towards different ends of the truck that they sat in, were lost in the thoughts of their house, their life, KASHMIR. As little Neha was asleep, Naina carefully rested her head on her lap and then the very first thing that striked her mind was what actually happened to them and all the the Kashmiri pandits in the valley. She went to the flashback. A December morning in 1889 it was. Everyone was asleep. It was dawn that that had covered the valley when all of a sudden the silence was broken. Some people had entered a house and had started firing. They threw stones from outside and broke the windows. The family had three children and their parents. The head of the family was killed as soon as he figured out what was happening and his wife along with the children tried to escape but were caught and shot eventually by the militants. Their screams, awakened the whole locality and everyone knew what had happened. There was terror, immense terror that now surrounded the valley and the Kashmiri pundits living there because next day it was out everywhere in the news that the sheer intention of these militants was to kill all the Kashmiri pandits in the valley who generally held higher positions as officers. Almost in no time darkness had surrounded Kashmir. It was no more the place which once used to be happy, where children used to play, where the Kashmiri pandit families would all be together and celebrate occasions in their large houses. When Rohan and Varun went to school the next day, they heard their teachers discussing about a bank being burnt by militants. Ninety percent of the employees working there were the pandits. Some of them had managed to escape but the others had lost their lives. Varun and Rohan were shocked. Later in the day, when Rohan was sitting in his class during a free period, they were all discussing about what happened in the last few days. There was a friend of his in the group named Iqbal who amidst this serious discussion suddenly said “if this continues to remain the case, then one day there will be no Kashmiri pandits left in Kashmir” and then he laughed. The rest of them in the group were all pandits and gave Iqbal a serious stare. For some reason, the situation had started to look like what Iqbal said. Just a few minutes to this conversation had passed when one of their teachers came to the classroom and informed them that the school had been dismissed because a stone fight had started across the city of Srinagar and militants were attacking the houses of the pandits with stones and were pelting stones on them wherever they saw them. At that time there were no school buses and children had to walk back from school to home. Amidst everything else, it was now a task for students of all the schools in the city to reach back home safely. All the children were tensed. All the students and teachers left the school right away. Rohan held Varun’s hand and they both started walking back to home slowly. They could not go through the main

road as it was risky and therefore chose the not so busy streets of the city to reach back home safely. Somehow they managed to not catch the eyes of the people who were throwing stones and managed to reach home on a safer note.

CHAPTER THREE

WHEN IT BEGAN

When they reached home, they only had had their grandparents and their little sister Neha at home because all the others were working. Megha and Naina were teachers in a school and Anand and Ambar worked in a company and a bank respectively where they were in good positions. In the evening, Megha and Naina reached home at the usual time. Anand joined in too. However, Ambar did not reach home at the normal time. All were tensed. Ambar generally reached back home by eight in the evening but today it was eleven and he had still not reached home. They all waited. The grandparents grew worried and started praying. Finally, at around twelve in the night, Ambar arrived, his shirt stained with blood. All became worried. They asked him about what had happened and he replied ' Luckily nothing happened to me but to a friend of mine.' He told them that when they were leaving the office and stepped out, they were attacked with stones by a few masked people. They all tried running and hiding back in the office when they caught their eye and those masked people entered their office and started attacking them. A friend of his named Avinash was brutally attacked and the attackers left leaving him wounded. Ambar and all his collegues went to drop Avinash to the hospital. It was because of this incident that he reached home late. Now the situation in the valley had worsened. They did not sleep that night. No Kashmiri pandit in the valley did. The night seemed longer than ever. They did not know what was awaiting them the next day. Next day in the morning it was announced that a curfew was put in Kashmir so that the situation could be brought in control. All the schools, colleges, banks, etc. were closed and all the people were informed to not leave their house because of the worsening conditions. No public transport facilities were available too. All of them stayed at home. Nobody went out. The valley was drenched in quietness that day when they all heard a ralley taking place outside. Some people shouted 'Throw Kashmiri Pandits out.' The intention was clear now. Everybody understood that the militants intended to throw Kashmiri pandits out of Kashmir and wanted to capture their houses and land. In the process, they did not even mind killing the pandits so that they held higher positions that the pandits did in government offices and also did so in order to clear the pandits out of the valley. The game had now begun. The scrutiny had begun. The intention of the militants was clear and so was their method. It was now violence that was chosen by them. That day, a friend of Ambar who was much younger came to their place. His name was Abdul. He was a little poor. When he came in, everybody in the family greeted him and welcomed him. Naina made him some tea. "So how is it that you came over after so long?"Ambar asked. "Actually I just needed some help. "Can you please lend me a pair of any of your old shoes so I can wear them to work. Actually I have not been able to buy one for the longest time now" said Abdul. "Oh its completely okay. I'll lend you a new pair of my shoes, wait let me get them" said Ambar. He gave a new pair of his shoes to Abdul and he thanked him. "Let me know if you need anything else. I understand the time is difficult" said Ambar smilingly. "Thank you so much" said Abdul and left as he was getting late. That entire day witnessed a day full of grief for the entire valley. The processions, the violence, any Kashmiri pandit seen on the road was shot dead by the militants without any delay or thought. This continued for a few days. The houses of many pandits were set on fire brutally during the night time. However, the curfew was opened after a few days so that everything could become normal. This, however, worsened the situation. The buses in which the pandits travelled were burnt and blown over continuously. One day, Megha had to go out for some important work, when she stepped into the bus, she realized that there were only men in the bus who seemed like the militants. She was scared but could not step down as if she did that the militants would know that she was a pandit and she could probably be attacked or shot. When she sat in the bus, she realized that all the men sitting in the bus, were looking at her. They probably realized that she was a Kashmiri pandit. When Megha saw this, she was scared but not scared enough to run out of her wits. She quickly removed the bindi that she wore on her forehead and covered her head with a stole so she could not look like who she actually was and resembled women from another community living in the valley. When the bus next stopped, she got down and started walking back home. Home was a little far, but she had no other option. On the way, she saw some terrorists who shot a man. No doubt he was a pandit. She saw them brutally dragging him out of his house and killing him but what could she do? She kept walking straight as she passed them with tears of fear in her eyes. But she stood brave and kept walking just when she heard one of those men calling her, "Madam". She stopped. She was scared. She feared that they recognized that she was a Kashmiri pandit. With all her courage, she looked back. The man came to her and said " Please don't come out of your house alone" he said in a low tone. "if any of my fellow counterparts would have recognized who you are, they would have killed you" and then he went. Maybe he saw the piece of jewellery every kashmiri pandit married woman wore in her ears and therefore, recognized her. Megha felt grateful that the idea of killing her did not cross the person's mind and that none of the other terrorists recognized her due to her disguised look. Finally, she kept walking and reached back home fear struck. Everybody at home had heard the news of buses in which Kashmiri pandits were travelling getting attacked and therefore, were worried thereafter. Now, it wasn't safe for anyone from the community to go out. In fact, their lives inside their own houses were risked. The happy times that they once spent seemed unapproachable.

CHAPTER FOUR

THE ALERT

Days passed, only to worsen the situation in the valley. Militancy reached its height. Nothing could really stop the problems. Everybody went to work but with hearts that were fear stricken. The houses were burned, the pandits were attacked and brutally killed. A hit-list was made. It consisted the names of those Kashmiri pandits who were next to be shot by the militants in the exact same order as they mentioned the names in the list. The militants entered the houses of these people and shot them dead. One of the cases was such that a person arrived at the house of a friend of his. His sister opened the door and greeted the person as he was her brother's friend. The person asked where his friend was. The sister told him that he was out and would arrive shortly. She asked him to have a seat while she would prepare tea for him. He agreed. She went to the kitchen and started making tea for her brother's friend. After a short while, she heard a very loud noise of a gunshot. She almost shook away. When she went out to see what had happened, she saw a stream of blood directed to the hall area. When she saw, it was her brother who was shot dead. There was no doubt who had shot him. Never could she have expected anything such from that person and nor could his brother have because they were both friends since childhood and had grown up playing together. Such was the brain wash done to such people in order to wipe the Kashmiri pandits out of Kashmir. The killed man's name was ticked in the hit-list as a record and mark that he was killed. Now, it was the turn of the others. The next one on the list was Mr. J.L Bhat who held a reputed position in a government office. Unfortunately, he wasn't even aware that his name was on the hit-list. The other day, when he was returning from his work, one of his fellow collegues who was not from his community stopped him over a brief chat. They both started talking. His collegue asked him about his plans of retirement. Mr.Bhat was surprised as to why his collegue had suddenly started talking about his retirement plans. When he asked him this, he replied that he knew that Mr. Bhat's children did not live in Kashmir and that he lived alone with his old wife. So he just wanted to give him a friendly advice of leaving the job and staying with his children in some other part of the country. Mr. Bhat became angry at this and said that he won't ever leave his land, his love, Kashmir and go and settle in some other part of the country. He then left. His collegue, then realized that he couldn't save his friend from his approaching end as he knew that his name was there on the hit-list but couldn't tell him directly about it as it would mean risking his own life as if the militants got to know that he had tried to warn a pandit against his approaching end, then the militants would kill him also. He felt sorry for the old man but knew that he did all he could to save his life, but all in vain. As he saw Mr.Bhat walking towards his home, he silently said " I will miss

you sir."

CHAPTER FIVE

THE UNCONVINCED

And then the other day, one could witness Mr. Bhat's name ticked in the hit-list. This was the time when all the pandits realized that it wasn't safe for them to live in their own land anymore. By this time, it was the year 1990 that had ringed in, the year of scrutiny, the year of grief, the year of pain. Everybody was scared but the will to cling on to their land bound all of them together and they decided not to be fearful. However, this belief seemed to be ending when such cases of brutal killing kept continuing. They all had big houses, lawns in which many different types of flowers and fruits grew, large lands, etc. But this wasn't the only reason why they did not want to leave the land, it was more because of the love that they had for their land which made them want not to leave it. It wasn't the snowfall that they would miss, it was playing together in the snow with everybody that they would miss. It wasn't the comfort of big houses, but the very fact of staying together that they would miss. No matter how much they wanted to be together, no matter how badly they wanted to be in their own land, there was something that constantly restricted them from holding within themselves, the very idea of spending the rest of their lives in the valley. It was a devil, a devil named TERRORISM. The next days witnessed many such killings.

CHAPTER SIX

THE HAUNT

There was another family with three daughters and their parents living together. While the daughters were young, their father held a reputed position in a government office. One night, the militants were at their door too. They banged the door right in the middle of the night and imagine the haunt in the hearts of the family members. The militants had come to shoot them dead.

CHAPTER SEVEN

THE CRY

They understood that something had come really close, something dangerous, something dreadful. There was a big room for storing grains in their house. It also had in it big drums to store rice. The mother immediately decided to save her daughters. She asked them to hide themselves in those drums. Then her husband too hid in the drum. By this time, the militants had broken the gates and had entered the house. There were four of them with rifles in their hands. Now, they searched each room of the house. They found the mother first. They asked her where the rest of the people of the house were. She did not answer even after continuously being questioned and threatened. So they dragged her by her hair, to every room in the house. Finally, when they went on to the second floor, they found the grain storage room. There they saw the drums and knew exactly where amidst the dark, the whole family had hidden. They did not even bother to open the drums for they knew everybody was hiding inside them. They started ruthless firing on the drums in front of the mother and all the three daughters along with their father were shot dead inside the drums itself. The mother cried as she could not do anything to

save her family and instead witnessed them dying despite several attempts of knocking the militants down and grabbing their hands and rifles with full force. After that, they shot her too and the whole family was killed in merely half an hour's time.

CHAPTER EIGHT

THE THREAT

The other morning, when everybody got to know about the incident, they were all fear stricken. Nobody knew who'd be the next person on target. Not only in any one particular city, but all the cities of Kashmir where the Kashmiri pandits lived, did their ruthless killing continue. Nobody knew when and how were the big houses of the Kahmiri pandits blown out by setting them on fire amidst the darkness of the nights. The family members were all killed in their own houses. Anybody of them seen out, were shot on the roads without any delay by the militants. Life for them, had become a game of terror. The cerfue was again imposed to get the situation in control, but all in vain. Processions were carried out with slogans of the pandits being washed out of the valley being shouted. Now, it was a threat to life, for any Kashmiri pandit family staying in the valley wasn't safe and could be killed anytime either by a gun shot or by their houses being set on fire. All the time, the threat of becoming a prey to the rifles of the militants haunted them. They all wanted to save their children and the family heads who held reputed positions in various offices as they were at the highest risk. Now, the time had

come. The time had come to leave the land and migrate in order to save their lives.

CHAPTER NINE

THE MOVE

The other day, in the valley of Srinagar, there lived a yet another Kashmiri pandit family. It was a family of four, the parents and their two children. Just next to their house, lived a family who were not pandits, but belonged to the other Kashmiri community living in Kashmir. They had a little daughter named Sehmat. She was just two years old and could barely speak, but could manage to speak a little bit, but not so clearly. She was a particular favourite to the Pandit family living next to them and the lady, in particular, was really fond of her. So Sehmat used to come to their house everyday and she used to feed her apples, walnuts, etc. everyday from the trees in their house garden. She used to love her a lot and also used to take great care of her. One day, like all the other days, Sehmat came to the lady's house to play. While her husband had gone to the office, she and her two daughters sat beside Sehmat to play with her. The lady fed her apples and as usual, held her close with love. Then, one of her daughters told Sehmat that she was really sweet and that they loved the fact that she used to come to play with them everyday. To this, Sehmat replied in Kashmiri in a rather unclear voice " But I wont be able to come tomorrow". "Why", asked the daughter, in a fun tone. "They will kill uncle tomorrow". "What?" asked the mother. At first they all thought that they hadn't heard her clearly so they asked her again, at which Sehmat starting singing in a nursery rhyme's tune " Uncle kill, family kill, Uncle kill, family kill". Now there was no doubt about what she meant. She had probably overheard her father's conversation with some people who were planning to kill the lady's husband and the whole family thereafter. They couldn't believe it but it was true. Then, Sehmat went back to her house, not realizing what she had said. That night, when the lady's husband came back home, they left the valley amidst the darkness of the night in order to save their life. They left in a hurry, and so did not carry anything along with them except for a few clothes as they did not have much time. Had they been noticed escaping, they would have been shot so they left immediately, not knowing that they would never return.

CHAPTER TEN

THE BETRAYAL

By this time, all the Kashmiri pandits in the valley had realized that they should leave and migrate to some other place or else they would be killed one by one. Staying anymore would mean risking their life. They had all decided to leave the valley to save their lives. They all starting leaving in the darkness of the nights so that they could not be seen by any of the militants because if they would have been seen, they would be killed. Just when they were all planning to leave, everyday new cases of houses of the pandits being set on fire and them being shot continued. However, by now they had starting leaving. For the older age group, it was worse than being killed but there was no option left. In some families, the grandparents denied leaving, they just could not tolerate the pain of separation, for a heartbreak is not merely when two people part ways, it is also when you go away from a place you loved and wished to spend your whole life in. With tears in their eyes and completely shattered souls, some of them did not even know that they couldn't even come back and eventually left. However, the killing continued. Some of them were even killed before they could leave or just when they were preparing to leave.

When militancy and terrorism was at its peak, finally Anand and Ambar too decided to leave along with the family. Yes, work was a priority, settlement too was, but not more than life. So on Megha and Naina's continous insistence, the family too had finally decided to leave. But they thought that they would return after the situation would cool down, so they decided to not carry much luggage along with them. It was Tuesday and they decided to leave the very next day so that they did not risk their lives any further. Since they had to leave the next day, they were all getting very emotional. Little Neha asked her dad, Ambar, why they were leaving to which Ambar replied that they had to take a new road, follow a new path. Little did Neha understand what Ambar said but since she heard the word 'road' and she knew that they were leaving tomorrow, she asked Ambar to take him out for a short walk. So, Ambar, along with Neha and Anand along with Rohan and Varun, went out for a short walk on the streets. It was quiet enough, yet pleasant. They could feel the scent of Kashmir which they knew they would miss. It was very peaceful over there. However, suddenly the peace and the calmness was hindered. They suddenly heard gunshots. Just when they heard rifles singing the song of terror, the got scared and tried returning towards home just when they saw five masked militants with guns in their hands. Obviously, they recognized them. Ambar and Anand started running back towards their house just when they heard a gunshot. The militants came running towards them and wanted to attack them. Anand and Ambar wanted to save the kids so they covered them and started running. Since they did not stop, the militants became impatient and one of them came closer to them and shot

Ambar on the leg. Luckily, he missed the aim but Ambar fell on the ground due to the panic. Anand helped him get up just when the masked militant tried shooting again but Anand held him by the hand and tried throwing his gun away. By this time, Ambar got up held little Neha, Varun and Rohan closer and told them to run towards home. Anand , however, somehow knocked the militant down so he fell on the ground. They were very scared. But the children did not run. So Anand and Ambar held them by hand, standing just next to the militant and told them to run just when little Neha told Ambar, “But daddy, those are your shoes.” He saw fear stricken and shocked. For a moment he froze. “I don’t believe this”, he said, then they all turned around and started running back towards home.

CHAPTER ELEVEN

THE UNBELIEVABLE

They knew that they were not safe, they had known that the militants want to wash the Kashmiri pandits off the valley, but little had they known that even the closest of their friends would betray them just because they were from the other community and wanted complete possession of Kashmir. After they reached back home, they were completely scared. Whatever happened was still expectable but, Ambar, was scarred. He could not believe it. His friend, Iqbal, had betrayed him. He couldn't have expected it. They were all shocked. The shoes he took from Ambar were the shoes he wore to carry out all the militant activities and moreover, to attack him and his family. Who had expected that the shoes he took from Ambar would be the ones he would wear to make the many pandit families run out of the valley.

CHAPTER TWELVE

THE ESCAPE

The next day, it was time. It was the day to leave Kashmir for them. The grandmother looked carefully at everything in the house, the walls, the floor, the thirteen rooms, the lawn, everything. She looked at them like she had never before. With tears in her eyes, and a heart that ached so much with the thought of leaving their house, she roamed around the entire house. It wasn't only her , but everybody in the family who looked at everything in the house so carefully like they had never seen it before. The kids were the younger ones, yet they could be seen touching everything in the house so carefully and observing everything more like they wanted to capture the last glimpse of the house and the essence of Kashmir forever in their eyes and heart. " Why are you all getting so upset?" asked Anand. "We will come back once everything becomes normal again. We can't leave our land like this."

CHAPTER THIRTEEN

THE FORCED EXILE

They had a huge house with thirteen rooms, a garden where fruits and vegetables grew and all the necessary items of necessity and luxury and so did most of the Kashmiri pandits, yet the only one thing that they felt bad about was the pain of leaving their land, there was too much of emotional attachment and too many memories that could not be forgotten. Finally now it was time, amidst the middle of the night, Anand and Ambar started loading a few items of necessity in a truck in which they would leave. They did not carry many things as deep in their hearts they had the belief that they would return and they quietly carried out the whole procedure. Megha and Naina covered their faces with their 'dupattas' . Then they all sat in the truck as soon as possible and in immense quietness gave their house and the streets a last look and left.

CHAPTER FOURTEEN

THE ACHE

And little Neha woke up from sleep and started crying. Her voice sort of got Naina back into senses, she shook her head that was leaning against the window, wiped off her tears and returned to the present from the flashback that was going on in her head. Now it was almost the morning. The sunlight could be witnessed peeping from behind the clouds, yet the darkness in their hearts could not be lightened up by anything. They had almost reached Jammu and now, the task was to find a place, a shelter to live. From living with luxury to being homeless, a new journey of the Kashmiri pandits had begun and now scrutiny and hardships awaited them. Now, they had reached Jammu. The problem was that they did not know where to go. With trunks and bags in their hands, they walked miles. The migration was a thing of immense sorrow but just a little sigh of relief that they could have was because the government at that time had organized the refugee camps for the migrants who migrated from Kashmir in such haste that they had absolutely nothing with them, not even the idea of a roof to shelter themselves with in this hard time. Finally, when they reached, they had to be registered. After getting registered, they were given a camp to live in, which was a tent like structure. Everybody who had migrated were given refuge over her. All Kashmiri pandits, shattered. And when they saw the tent that they had to all with full family live in, they were broken. From large houses to a tent to live in with the whole family, from well settled to homeless, from a native to a REFUGEE in their own country, the life of Kashmiri pandits took a drastic turn, a vulnerable situation the ache of which knew no bounds, absolutely none.

CHAPTER FIFTEEN

THE NOISE

But what could they do. They had to now live in camps with their whole families which weren't even half as big as a room in their houses in Kashmir. There was noise, noise all around. Not the one that was made by people, but the one which was going on in their heads. The noise that left all the Kashmiri pandits shattered, the shouts, the screams of the pandit families who had brutally been killed, begging for life, begging to stay. Some couldn't even leave. Some continued to stay because they wanted to take their last breaths in the holy land of Kashmir. Here, living in the camps, they all met, talked to each other about what happened to them, shared each others' pain and remembered the life of Kashmir. The life here was much different and to be precise, much difficult. They had to all live in small camps along with the whole family, work on their own without any help and only with items of necessity and most importantly, look for new jobs to earn a living and run the family. Only the ones who already owned a house in Jammu or had built one in some other part of the country, certainly did not face much hardship searching for a roof to live under. When there are so many people living together, there is a mixture of emotions that can be felt with everyone coming up with their own story of hardships and terror. One could witness such stories in these refugee camps for years.

CHAPTER SIXTEEN

THE CHANGE

By this time the scrutiny of the Kashmiri pandits and the migration incident was out in the media and everyone got to know about the riots that had taken place in Kashmir and how the Kashmiri pandits were forced to leave their land and migrate because of their brutal killing that was taking place in the valley. But, the Kashmiri pandits continued to stay in hardship for years and some, forever. A few days after the migration had taken place, someone approached Anand. He was one of their relatives named Nitin who came there and asked Anand to come and stay with them till the time they found some other place to maybe rent and live in. he said that with them owning a house, he did not want Anand and his family to live in a camp especially after knowing how hard life was there. Anand first denied but Nitin insisted so they finally agreed to go live in his house till the time they could find a job and afford to rent a place to live in. So they went with him to live in his house. This was the case with many Kashmiri pandits who owned a house in Jammu already that they had the families of their relatives living with them for a very long time till their relatives found some other place to live. Three to four families would live in a single house. Some would sleep on the terrace, some in the verandah, some in the lawn (if they had one) and some congested in different rooms in the house. When it would rain, the flood of water would invade the house and get along with it lots of dirt and at times, insects too. This wasn't all, since they were all pretty used to colder weather, they could also at times not bear the heat. And the only upgrade for the ones living in the camps years later was that they got small government quarters to live in even after so many years.

CHAPTER SEVENTEEN

THE DARE

As for Anand, Ambar and their whole family, when they came over to Nitin's place, after a few days, they decided to get some of their other belongings which they needed and had left back in their house in Kashmir because they thought that they would return. However, the situation in the valley was worsening and terrorism reached its height so they realized there was no way they could go back ever again. So, now, they decided to get some of their precious belongings that they left in Kashmir here. Anand, Ambar, Megha and Naina left for this leaving the children and the grandparents at Nitin's house. They went via bus from Jammu to Kashmir. Two days passed and there was no news from the latter. There were no mobile phones at that time so they could not hear from them. Just then, the news of firing at the bus stands of Kashmir broke everywhere. The militants did firing on the buses at the bus stand which came from Jammu and many people travelling in them had become prey to the gun shots and died. The children, grandparents and Nitin's family, all became really tensed. There was no word from them so they could not even eat and sleep properly because they did not know how and where

Anand, Ambar, Megha and Naina would be. A week passed and there was no news from them. They did not want to but were now, somehow convinced that maybe they were shot too. The grandmother cried because despite an already aching heart because of leaving Kashmir, she could not now bear the loss of her kids. Little Neha started crying too. Nitin and her wife consoled the grandmother and told her that everything will be alright. “This old heart can no longer bear the pain of separation any more”, she said crying. They were all messed up and did not know what to do. All they could do was to wait for some news .

CHAPTER EIGHTEEN

THE UNEXPECTED

The next day, when they woke up from sleep in the morning, there they were, Anand, Ambar, Megha and Naina. They were standing in front of the main gate of the house. Nitin's wife saw them and opened the gate. She was really happy to see them safe. When they entered the house, the happiness of the grandparents and the children knew no bounds. Nitin's wife served them water and then Nitin asked them what had happened and what took them so long to reach back. Ambar told him that the day the buses from Jammu at the bus stand were being fired upon, they too were sitting in one of the buses. However, they managed to escape somehow and reached their home, grabbed everything that they needed as fast as possible and left, but because the militants had an eye on every bus that left for Jammu so that they could shoot the Kashmiri pandits travelling in them, the four of them waited for the situation to cool down a bit and stayed over at one of Anand's friend's house who was not a Kashmiri pandit so that they could be safe as living in their own house for even a few days would have meant risking their lives. After the situation became a little cool, they immediately left for Jammu. “What a terrible place it seemed like. As if it wasn’t our Kashmir. As if it was some dark land.”, Ambar said.

CHAPTER NINETEEN

THE SEARCH

Now, because they could all not live in Nitin's house forever, Megha and Naina used to walk miles daily in the hot sun in order to search for a house, or for that matter even a room to rent and live in. On the other hand, Anand and Ambar had started looking for new jobs to start earning again. After they found a two room place to rent, they started living there. They had now become habitual to living in small places. They were not habitual to living in small places but eventually they learned to adjust. Here they had to live as per the guidelines set by the landlord who lived with his family on the ground floor. They felt like they were no more their own masters and so did all the Kashmiri pandits. All the hardships that they faced, everything that they came across, they kept on dealing with it beautifully without complaining, yet every heart remembered Kashmir, wanted to go back to Kashmir but they couldn't. This time witnessed many Kashmiri pandits, especially the older ones dyeing of the shock and grief of leaving their land and seeking refuge in their own country while facing such hardships. The others might be smiling, but deep inside, they all cried every night remembering what happened to them. Life

for all of them, just went on with scars of separation.

CHAPTER TWENTY

DARK

None of them could for years forget the terror instilled in their hearts as a result of the massive killings and terrorism in Kashmir. In nights, they couldn't sleep. What had happened was bad. The situation haunted them. The tough times that they were facing, leaving behind any trace of comfort, happiness, etc. that once filled their life, broke them down. They were shocked, shocked to no extent. No matter how much they all tried, they somehow just couldn't move on, especially, the older section. They couldn't adjust to a place that was so different from what they had seen all their lives. Who had thought that the people who lived in large house and were well off and educated, who lived with comfort and luxury had to one day live in a single room with their whole family facing all the hardships for no sin of their own.

CHAPTER TWENTY-ONE

THE SUNSET

Two years later, Anand and Ambar bought a new flat in Delhi and started living there. It was a two BHK flat . the Kashmiri pandit families who could later afford to buy houses did so but the ones who had left in worse conditions and could not afford to buy a house of their own, continued to live in the small quarters provided to them by the government. The scrutiny was immense, the pain was unbearable, the place Kashmir held in their hearts was irreplaceable, but they continued to live. They knew that the wish of taking their last breath in Kashmir was unapproachable and therefore, continued to hold their souls in their body for as long as they could sustain them, yet there was no day when the thought of Kashmir and all the fun and frolic they had over there, did not cross their mind for atleast once.

CHAPTER TWENTY-TWO

THE LEAP

Time flew, Years passed, so did a few situations and so did a lot of lives. The Kashmiri pandits had a culture of their own, traditions of their own. They did not let themselves forget them. They taught their children about their rituals, tradition, culture and festivals. The Shivratri puja, for instance, is one such major festival of theirs which they continued to celebrate with full zeal every year no matter how hard situations had turned out for them to be. They did not give up on their culture, the only difference being the fact that now, years after the migration had taken place, they had now also incorporated the value of celebrating festivals like Holi and many others, which they did not celebrate with as much zeal and enthusiasm as they do now. Despite all the changes that took place in their life, they did not give up on their own values and traditions and continued to raise their children with knowledge of the same.

CHAPTER TWENTY-THREE

WALKING THE FLOOR AGAIN

Twenty years passed. In the year 2010, Anand and Ambar decided to revisit Kashmir with the whole family. The children had now grown. They could barely remember anything about Kashmir now and were keen on this trip so they could see the land of their birth, their origin, yet again. The grandparents had grown even older, not because of the time that had passed, more because of the pain they had been holding in their heart ever since migration took place. Not even a single day in the last twenty years had passed without witnessing tears of separation of their home rolling down their eyes. Now, when after twenty years, they got the opportunity of visiting Kashmir again, they couldn't contain their happiness. They travelled via road so they could not miss upon any little thing that came on the way. They wanted to see everything, wanted to feel everything. When they reached Kashmir, their happiness knew no bounds. Even before reaching the hotel that would stay in, Anand asked the taxi driver to drive them to Pehelgam first, the place where they lived, the place where their house was and of course, the place they had spent their whole childhood in. They were all very excited. After some time of driving, when they still didn't reach, Ambar asked the driver " How much more time will it take to reach Pehelgam?". "We are in Pehelgam already sir", said the driver. "This is Pehelgam?", he asked in a shocked voice. " Yes sir, we are now driving towards your house as you had said". "Sorry we could not recognize" said Ambar continuously looking out of the window in surprise. "It's completely alright sir, a lot has changed here since 1990", said the driver.

CHAPTER TWENTY-FOUR

THE AMAZEMENT

All of them were continuously looking out of the window in amazement because the place had changed so much that they couldn't even recognize it despite having their whole childhood spent there. Finally, they reached their house, the house that they once lived in, the house that held so many memories. They all stepped out of the taxi with their eyes continuously directed towards the house. Not even for a moment did they take their eyes off the house. It had changed so much. Somebody else had started living there. They walked around the entire boundary of the house with tears in their eyes remembering all the days they had spent there. The grandmother, continuously kept on touching the walls of the house. After twenty long years, was she back to her house and had touched the walls of the house she had spent a huge part of her life in. The children looked at the house in such amazement because it was now so different from what they had left it to be. They all had tears in their eyes and with immense strength, Anand knocked the main door of the house. An old man, nearly eighty years of age, opened the door. When he saw the family, he was shocked. He recognized the grandparents. Anand asked him if they could just for some time come in and see the house. He promised to not take much time. The old man said, "It's your house. Come in." They all went in. The old man's family now lived there so they did not feel much comfortable but they walked around the whole house with each room reminding them of the time spent there. They couldn't control weeping looking at how much everything had changed. Now they did not want to spend much time there because they knew being there for too long would mean hurting themselves emotionally. So they had a look around the house and then left. When they were leaving, Varun picked up some soil from the lawn, kept it in his pocket and then they all sat in the taxi and went towards the hotel. On the way, Megha saw her parents' house. The house that she had spent her whole childhood in. It was down in ashes now. It was burnt down completely. Such a beautiful house it used to be once, all ruined now. The more important thing was that had it not been this place, she wouldn't even have recognized her own house. Almost all the houses in that area that once belonged to the Kashmiri pandits were all blown and burnt. Nothing except a mere structure could be seen now with eyes full of nothing but tears. "Oh my dear valley, we've missed you so much", cried her heart. They reached the hotel after that and decided to rest for the day and roam around a little on the next day. The other day in the morning, when Naina went to her grandmother to wake her up for breakfast, she did not wake. She tried everything she could but the grandmother did not wake. She knew what had happened. The contentment on the grandmother's face was immense. This is the only thing she was waiting for, to be back in her land. To be in Kashmir again and take her last breath there was what had made her cling on to her life for last so many year. Her last breathe was in the holy land of Kashmir and its satisfaction could clearly be seen on her old face. None of them cried. They were happy, happy because the grandmother had achieved what she wanted, to be found somewhere on the land of Kashmir at the end of her life. After a week, they all went back to Delhi. On the way back, looking outside the window with his head slightly out, feeling the serenity of the land and the air of Kashmir, Anand slowly said " Ae vaadi, tu bhool toh nahi jaayegi na humein?"

9 798889 751649

Printed by Libri Plureos GmbH in Hamburg,
Germany